HOME AND DRY

HOME AND DRY

MIKE PEYTON

FERNHURST BOOKS

First published 1989 by
Fernhurst Books, 31 Church Road, Hove
East Sussex

ISBN 0 906754 48 8

Design by Gaye Allen
Composition by
Screenset Typesetting, Seaford
Printed by Hollen Street Press, Slough.

Printed and bound in Great Britain

To those who recognise themselves in any of these drawings.

Acknowledgements

These cartoons are published with the kind permission of *Yachts & Yachting, Practical Boat Owner* and *Yachting Monthly,* where they first appeared.

CONTENTS

—1—
OFFSHORE

'Bacon well done Joe?'

'The Coastguard says the Lifeboat is on its way.
Just put the kettle on and relax . . . '

'It was frightfully decent of you to try and help us.'

'I can't find what "continuous short blasts" *mean in Reeds.'*

'It's going to take a bit of re-adjusting to the old Enterprise
on the gravel pit.'

'Are you sure we're hard on the wind?'

'I don't know about scattering his ashes on the sea; he's going to be back on shore before us.'

'What the hell do you mean, "It can't happen"? It has!'

'I can't understand it, you've been like a wet blanket ever since that sailing holiday in Greece.'

'*How's this, and to hell with the number of words:*
Must sell, comfortable, sea kindly, well-loved ketch . . . ?'

'Who said fishermen don't wave to yotties?'

—2—
YACHTMASTERS ALL

'Never mind going below to check, what do I do?'

'It's very satisfactory when they turn up dead on the nose like the
"West Knock" there.'

'That's the beacon all right, it always has cormorants on it.'

*'What do you mean, "When she's on automatic you rely on
the 30-metre error"?'*

'There you are — I've got the waypoints of every pub
on the south coast in its memory.'

'They want to know if we've got the "East Sunk" on board.'

'My position? On top of the doghouse.'

'You shouldn't have gone to the trouble, Commodore.
Annie does all our navigation — she's a wizard with Decca.'

'Keep the beacon well to port and we'll be fine.'

'I agree with you darling, it should be The Owers.'

—3—
ROUND THE CANS

'If he goes on again about the windshift that only he saw from the back of the fleet — and he won — I'll do him.'

'*Tack as usual, whenever you hear a snore.*'

'I'll give even money it's a class V, twenty to one a class I.'

'Caroline thinks we're stupid.'

'I know I said drop it smartly. But not that bloody smartly.'

'My lot slept on board, so they'll be bright-eyed and . . . '

'We're not going. We've got no-one who understands
the electronics.'

— 4 —
BACK AT THE YARD

'Well, you're always telling me how you prefer gardening.'

'You've caught us at rather a busy moment, Mr Fairhall.'

*'Relax, relax, there'll be nothing coming up the river
so late on the tide.'*

'Sophie, darling, don't touch that.'

'I know she'll take up, but will the engine?'

'Tea, darling.'

'We're after the pricey stuff — brass screws, stainless shackles . . .'

—5—
THE LADIES

'It's a funny old sky, and with that forecast and women and
children it's difficult to decide what's the best thing to do.'

'Yes we have; we're inflating it now.'

'But you're not due back till the weekend!'

'But darling, normally you like photos of your boat!'

'As you were, darling. A white flasher on the north pier is for vessels leaving harbour.'

'Seems a pity to use expensive flares; the box says they were five and sixpence each.'

'Sorry to be so long darling, I'll only be a few more minutes.'

'How's your bad back?'

'No wonder you couldn't find them darling, they're all here!'

'That's the last time you talk me into sailing around to the
annual dinner dance.'

'Typical of your mother: right in the middle of Burnham Week.'

—6—
ALL ASHORE

'Port watsch upschtanding.'

'Bloody bait diggers.'

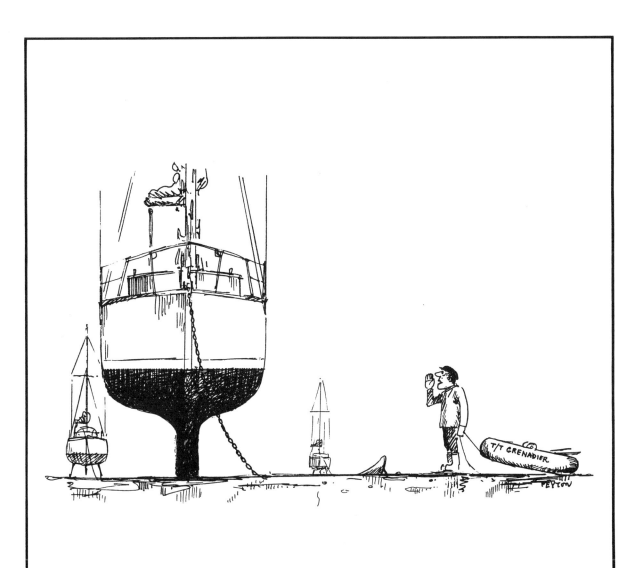

'Darling, don't move.'

'I can never understand the song and dance some of them make
about fitting out. I just give the yard carte blanche.'

'Generally I go through the Straits of Magellan.'

'Hey, I've just picked up a Mayday.'

'A bit pretentious — letting us know it wasn't his fault.'

—7—
ON A TALL SHIP

'I don't know about my moral fibre, but it's certainly done a lot for my sense of self-preservation.'

PEYTON

'Messenger, go and tell the Skipper there's broken water ahead.'

'Call yourselves yachtsmen and you can't tell a staysail haly . . . !'

'Where shall I put my things?'

—8—
SAFE IN HARBOUR

*'Beats me why they operate harbour signals for
small boats like that!'*

It's a good weight carrier you said, takes four easily.'

'Do you think they're trying to tell us something?'

'I think you're optimistic if you think that a bottle of Scotch will be all they'll want.'

'You bloody fool, why didn't you write this one off?'

'Go easy with that French courtesy flag, John.'

'There's nothing wrong with <u>his</u> navigation.'

'I always hug the harbour head, it's safer.'

—9—
CLOSE INSHORE

'Absolutely disgusting, no moral standards whatever.'

'Moored boat dead ahea . . . '

'I thought you did all this at night school — working out tides, times, ranges . . . '

'Let's read those instructions again, Joe.'

'We're not the only ones with problems. That big ketch behind is dragging, and fast.'

'And next time you're going to sail your anchor out, let us know
and we'll all move first.'

'It's very decent of you . . .
I'm afraid we're the last boat on the moorings.'

'Stuffed the oars under the forward bunk did you?
I know where I'd like to stuff them!'

'He must be below. He's not on deck.'

'I don't think this bar is as bad as the Pilot makes . . . '

'Coastguard, Coastguard, this is yacht Anticipation. *I'm not actually in trouble now but . . . '*

'Have a nice day!'

ALSO PUBLISHED BY FERNHURST BOOKS

HUMOUR

Still Wet Behind the Ears   *Lesley Black &*
  Mike Peyton
Windsurfing   *Frank Fox*
Ski with Peyton   *Mike Peyton*

YACHTING

Celestial Navigation   *Tom Cunliffe*
Weather at Sea   *David Houghton*
Inshore Navigation   *Tom Cunliffe*
Marine VHF Operation   *Michael Gale*
Heavy Weather Cruising   *Tom Cunliffe*
Yacht Skipper   *Robin Aisher*
Yacht Crewing   *Malcolm McKeag*
Tuning Yachts and Small Keelboats   *Lawrie Smith*
Motor Boating   *Alex McMullen*
Simple Electronic Navigation   *Mik Chinery*
Children Afloat   *Pippa Driscoll*

SAILING

Sailing: A Beginner's Manual   *John Driscoll*
Racing: A Beginner's Manual   *John Caig &*
  Tim Davison
Sailing the Mirror   *Roy Partridge*
Mirror Racing   *Guy Wilkins*
Topper Sailing   *John Caig*
The Laser Book   *Tim Davison*
Laser Racing   *Ed Baird*
Boardsailing: A Beginner's Manual   *John Heath*
Board Racing   *Geoff Turner & Tim Davison*
The Catamaran Book   *Brian Phipps*
Knots & Splices   *Jeff Toghill*

SAIL TO WIN

Tactics   *Rodney Pattisson*
Dinghy Helming   *Lawrie Smith*
Dinghy Crewing   *Julian Brooke-Houghton*
Wind Strategy   *David Houghton*
Tuning Your Dinghy   *Lawrie Smith*
The Rules in Practice   *Bryan Willis*
Tides and Currents   *David Arnold*
Boatspeed — Supercharging your hull,
  foils and gear   *Rodney Pattisson*
Sails   *John Heyes*
The Winning Mind — Strategies for
  successful sailing   *John Whitmore*

If you would like to receive regular information
about our new and forthcoming books, please send
your name and address to:

Fernhurst Books, 31 Church Road, Hove,
East Sussex BN3 2FA